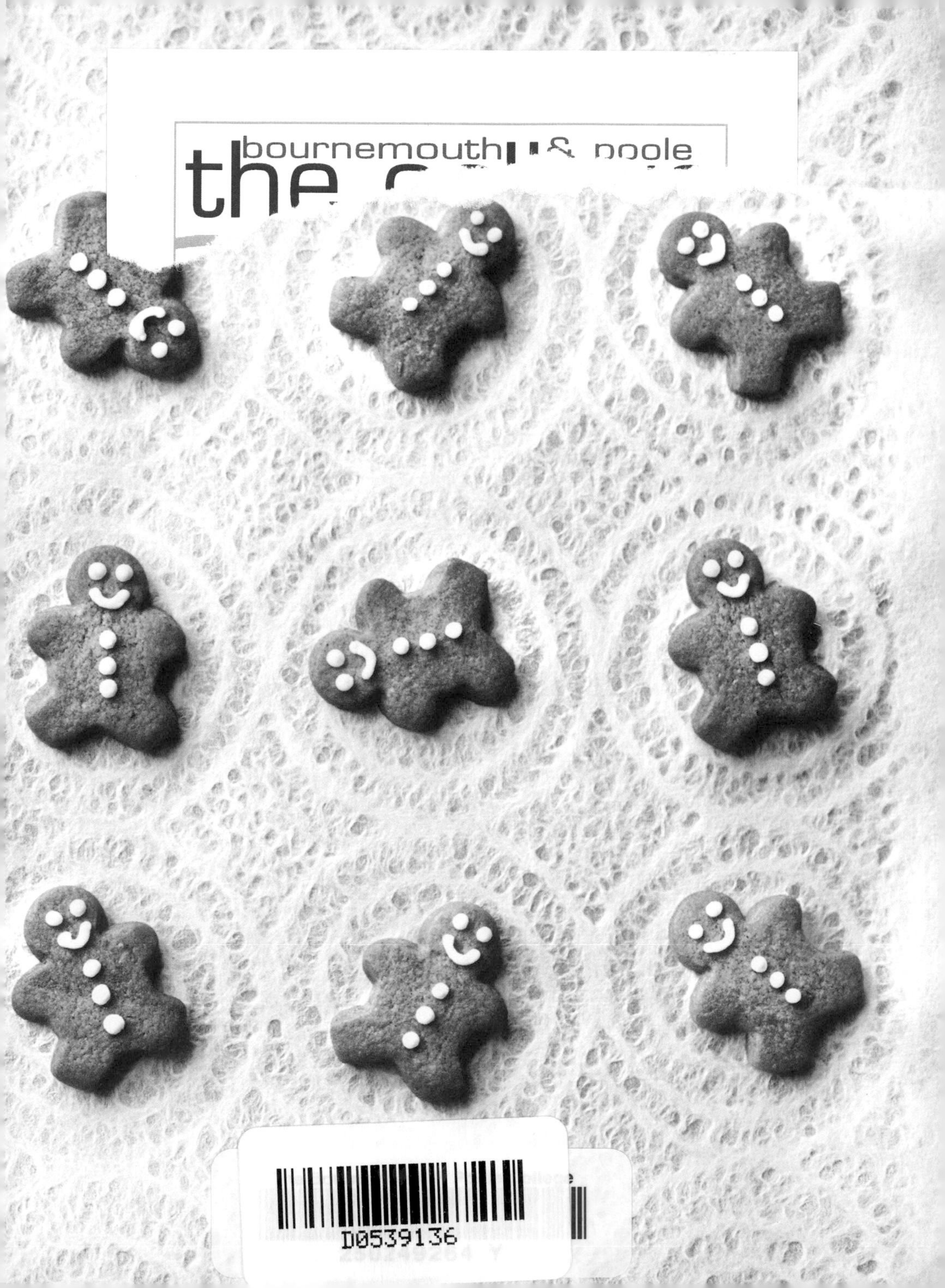

GINGER BREAD
WONDERLAND

FOR TOM

When your tummy rumbles at teatime,
it's natures way of telling you to eat more biscuits.

GINGER BREAD WONDERLAND

30 MAGICAL BISCUITS, BAKES & HOUSES

★ MIMA SINCLAIR ★

First published in Great Britain in 2015 by
Kyle Books, an imprint of Kyle Cathie Ltd
192-198 Vauxhall Bridge Road
London SW1V 1DX
general.enquiries@kylebooks.com
www.kylebooks.com

10 9 8 7 6 5 4 3 2 1

ISBN 978 0 85783 320 4

Designer: Anita Mangan
Photographer: Tara Fisher
Food Stylist: Mima Sinclair
Prop Stylist: Tabitha Hawkins
Project Editor: Sophie Allen
Editorial Assistant: Hannah Coughlin
Production: Nic Jones, Gemma John and Lisa Pinnell

A Cataloguing in Publication record for this title is available
from the British Library.

Colour reproduction by ALTA London
Printed and bound in Singapore by Tien Wah Press

CONTENTS

INTRODUCTION

I love baking. My knees go weak at the sight of a chewy biscuit or a light sponge. More icing goes in my mouth than makes it onto its intended counterpart. I blame my mum, she spoiled us with homemade biscuits and bakes after school. Coming home to a house still full of the heady scent of baked goods is something that doesn't leave you. Friends at school would always want to come to our house at the weekend because the kitchen wasn't banned, it was our playground.

So my love affair with sweet treats has grown up with me, it's moulded me, it's comforted me and the comfort I have felt has happily spread to others. That's the joy of baking, people are thrilled by it. I like to feed those around me with all the sweet delights that I get so much excitement out of baking, and they eagerly receive them. I get just as much joy from sharing goodies as I do gobbling them all up myself!

This collection of recipes has something for everyone's tastes and suits a variety of baking abilities. Packed with a range of classic and contemporary recipes, you have all you need to turn your kitchen into a gingerbread wonderland. Bake perfect treats to slip into lunch boxes, serve up to friends at tea, give as gifts or have as a festive centrepiece. Turn up at a party with a gingerbread house and you are sure to be at the top of everyone's invite lists next year!

I hate recipes that need lots of complicated equipment and hard-to-source ingredients. The ingredients used in these recipes are basic and inexpensive, as are the little bits of equipment you will need along the way. Most of these things you will probably already have in your store cupboard, but please heed my advice in the dough tips about old spices. New cutters don't have to be bought – use what you have or create your own from thick card, using my templates (see pages 96–109).

Follow my tips on dough, baking and piping to avoid mistakes and achieve your best-ever bakes. A word of advice – don't sweat the small stuff. Who cares if your piping isn't straight, your gingerbread house is on the wonk or something didn't turn out exactly the way you meant it – mine doesn't always and that's the magic of it being homemade. I guarantee your efforts will still be met with wide greedy eyes and you will soon enjoy the beautiful silence that only comes from a room of contented people whose mouths are full. Now get in the kitchen and have some fun!

LIGHT
GINGERBREAD DOUGH

MAKES 1KG · PREP: 10 MINUTES, PLUS 1 HOUR 15 MINUTES CHILLING · COOK: 5 MINUTES

This is a mild and sweet, light dough that is very versatile.

140g light molasses/
golden syrup or honey
200g soft light brown sugar
200g unsalted butter
zest of 1 unwaxed lemon
4 teaspoons ground ginger
2 teaspoons
ground cinnamon
½ teaspoon ground nutmeg
¼ teaspoon ground cloves
1 teaspoon
bicarbonate of soda
500g plain flour
1 teaspoon salt
1 lightly beaten medium
free-range egg

1. Pour the light molasses into a large saucepan with the sugar, butter, zest and spices and melt over a low/medium heat, stirring frequently until the sugar has dissolved.

2. Increase the heat to bring the mixture to boiling point. Remove from the heat and beat in the bicarbonate of soda. The mixture will froth up at this point as the bicarbonate reacts – mix briefly until combined, then leave to cool for 15 minutes.

3. Sift the flour and salt, then fold into the mixture in batches, using a wooden spoon or a stand mixer. Beat in the egg using a wooden spoon or a stand mixer, until just combined. Do not overwork the mixture, or the biscuits will spread during baking.

4. The dough will be very sticky to begin with, but do not add any flour. Scrape out of the bowl onto a clean surface and knead together until just smooth. Wrap in cling film and chill in the fridge for 1 hour.

DARK GINGERBREAD DOUGH

MAKES 1KG - PREP: 10 MINUTES, PLUS 1 HOUR 15 MINUTES CHILLING - COOK: 5 MINUTES

A stronger, spicier dough and visually darker because of the use of dark molasses.

80g dark molasses/
black treacle

60g light molasses/
golden syrup or honey

200g soft dark
brown sugar

200g unsalted butter

zest of ½ unwaxed
orange

4 teaspoons
ground ginger

2 teaspoons
ground cinnamon

½ teaspoon
ground nutmeg

¼ teaspoon
ground cloves

1 teaspoon
bicarbonate of soda

500g plain flour

1 teaspoon salt

1 lightly beaten
medium free-range egg

1. Pour the dark and light molasses into a large saucepan with the sugar, butter, zest and spices and melt over a low/medium heat, stirring frequently until the sugar has dissolved.

2. Increase the heat to bring the mixture to boiling point. Remove from the heat and beat in the bicarbonate of soda. The mixture will froth up at this point as the bicarbonate reacts – mix briefly until combined, then leave to cool for 15 minutes.

3. Sift the flour and salt, then fold into the mixture in batches, using a wooden spoon or a stand mixer. Beat in the egg using a wooden spoon or stand mixer, until just combined. Do not overwork the mixture, or the biscuits will spread during baking.

4. The dough will be very sticky to begin with, but do not add any flour. Scrape out of the bowl onto a clean surface and knead together until just smooth. Wrap in cling film and chill in the fridge for 1 hour.

TIP

If using honey in either recipe then be aware that it can cause your dough to spread a little when baked.

BASICS

ALLERGIES & INTOLERANCES

No one should ever be deprived of baked goods. It is just not fair! Whether you are intolerant or allergic to certain produce all is not lost. There is a fantastic range of 'free from' products available in most large supermarkets or health food stores. They taste great and will allow you to enjoy your sweet treats once again. Simply substitute the 'free from' equivalent into the recipes in place of items you must avoid.

Gluten free

Gluten-free flour is usually a blend of rice, potato, tapioca, maize and buckwheat flours. Making your own is possible, but mixed blends can be bought easily at the supermarket or health food stores. You may find that the dough is a little drier when using gluten-free flour so add a little extra golden syrup or black treacle to moisten it.

Dairy free

Dairy-free alternatives to butter, milk and cream can be easily substituted, such as sunflower spread, coconut oil, soya, almond, hazelnut or rice milk.

Egg free

With the biscuits it is possible just to leave the egg out. The dough is a little crumbly to work with but still manageable - try rolling out between two pieces of greaseproof paper for best results. The result will be a snappier biscuit, but it will still taste delicious. You can also substitute with dried egg replacement powder, just follow the packet instructions for quantities to substitute per egg. For any egg washes, substitute with oil, milk or dairy-free milk.

MOLASSES

Molasses is traditionally used in gingerbread as it adds a rich and spicy flavour to baked goods. The term molasses covers any uncrystallised syrups that are a by-product of the sugar-making process. The juice extracted from sugar cane is boiled until some of the sugars crystallise. This juice is then boiled numerous times to extract as much sugar as possible. The thick and sweet syrup that is left is molasses.

The most common types of molasses are the pale syrups known as light molasses and the darker syrups known as black or dark treacle and blackstrap molasses.

Light molasses

This is the syrup resulting from the first cooking of the sugar cane. Amber in colour and similar in appearance to honey. It has the highest sugar content and mildest flavour of the molasses.

Black/dark treacle molasses

From the second cooking of the sugar cane, dark molasses is slightly thicker and darker in colour and has a slightly bitter, richer and less sweet flavour.

Blackstrap molasses

From the third cooking of the sugar cane, blackstrap molasses is very concentrated and therefore is the darkest, least sweet of all the molasses with a distinctively strong, almost pungent flavour.

I use both light and dark molasses to create two distinguishable colours and strengths of gingerbread. The light dough will give you light golden biscuits with a mild, sweet flavour. The dark dough will give you a dark biscuit with a stronger, spicier flavour.

The different colour doughs can be used to enhance your bakes – so think about how you will decorate your biscuits or house when picking your dough recipe, and choose the shade that will compliment it best.

DOUGH TIPS

1. Dough can be made in advance and stored in the fridge allowing time for the spices to permeate the dough. If left for more than a couple of hours in the fridge, you will need to rest the dough at room temperature for 10-20 minutes on the side to soften slightly before rolling.

2. Do not over-mix the dough once you have added the egg as it will become quite sticky and difficult to remove from the bowl. Mix it until just combined because this develops the gluten in the dough to make the biscuits chewy. Over-mixing will create a tougher end result. However, if it does become sticky just use a spatula to scrape the dough into a freezer bag and chill as usual.

3. Chilling the dough is an important step. It makes it more pliable and easier to shape.

4. Always chill again in the fridge or freezer after rolling and cutting out the dough. This keeps the biscuits from spreading too much and losing their shape.

5. You can use spice mixes such as: English mixed spice, American pumpkin pie spice, or Dutch speculaas spice in place of the spices I have included in the recipes. Add up the quantity of individual spices in the recipe and replace the total amount with your spice mix.

6. Using up old spices from the back of the cupboard sounds like a great idea but on average whole spices only stay fresh for 4 years and ground spices for only 2 years. Buying better quality and fresher spices rather than just what is available at the supermarket will result in a better flavour in your baking. Try specialist whole food stores or ethnic markets where demand is higher so restocking is more frequent. Consider buying whole spices and grinding them yourself so that you can retain maximum flavour and potency. Store your spices away from direct light or heat and keep tightly closed.

7. Using cutters, plastic or metal, will yield a sharper edge and a more uniform batch of biscuits than making your own templates and cutting each out. However, sometimes you can't get hold of the right cutter for the job. Then it's best to draw your desired shape onto thick card and cut out using a small sharp scalpel. Use a new blade or a knife tip to cut out the dough, making sure the dough is well chilled before cutting to avoid it sticking as it takes longer to cut by hand.

BAKING TIPS

1. Longer cooking times will yield stiffer biscuits, so if you are constructing a house or something similar that needs support, cook until a little more golden than you might an individual biscuit.

2. Use spacers to roll out your dough for perfect, even thickness every time. They can be found in bakeware stores or simple slats of wood cut to size work just as well.

3. Ovens can run hot or cold. I recommend a test bake of a small tray of biscuits before baking the whole batch to check the true baking times. Alternatively, buy a small oven thermometer. They are inexpensive and can be a very useful piece of kit for baking.

4. I have used a lower oven temperature to bake my biscuits than you might find in other baking books. I found this helped the dough to hold it's shape well, and allowed the biscuits to cook through entirely without overcooking the surface.

5. For best results, bake a single sheet of biscuits in the centre of the oven. If baking batches, set racks in the upper and lower thirds of the oven and rotate the trays from top to bottom during baking.

ICING & PIPING

ROYAL ICING

MAKES 300G

250g icing sugar
1 lightly beaten medium egg white
½ teaspoon lemon juice
1 teaspoon water

1. Sift the sugar into the bowl of an electric mixer. Add the beaten egg white and lemon juice.

2. Whisk on a low speed, so you do not incorporate too much air into the icing, for 2–3 minutes until you have a smooth, but not wet, stiff peak consistency. It should be dense and spreadable but hold a stiff peak. If it looks dry and crumbly add a little water. If it looks slightly runny and glossy, add a little extra icing sugar.

3. You now have stiff peak icing for sticking houses together and placing decorations onto icing. Transfer to a bowl and cover with a damp cloth to prevent it from drying out. The icing can be prepared ahead and stored in an airtight container in the fridge for up to 1 week.

You can adjust this icing to make soft peak and flood icing:

- Soft peak – Add a drop of water at a time until you have icing that holds a soft peak but does not spread on its own. Use for piping lines, borders and decorations.

- Flood icing – Add a teaspoon of water at a time until you have a thick but runny icing that smoothes out on its own within 15 seconds but not so runny that it runs off the edge of your biscuit. Use for filling in outlined areas of biscuits.

Each recipe will give directions on which type of icing you will need.

TIPS

1. If you have no piping bags make your own by twisting a tight cone out of baking parchment, or use a small plastic food bag and cut one corner off.

2. If you do not have piping nozzles you can just cut the end of the piping bag off. Note that a nozzle will give you better results as you have more control.

3. Only half fill the piping bag with icing so it does not ooze out of the top when you squeeze.

4. To make chocolate icing, substitute 60g of cocoa powder in place of an equal amount of icing sugar.

PIPING TIPS

1. Cut the end off your piping bag and insert a small plain round piping nozzle.

2. Half fill your piping bag with icing, then twist the top of the bag. Secure the end in the hand you are piping with.

3. Touch the starting point with the tip of the piping bag and slowly squeeze out the icing. As you squeeze, lift the bag slightly so you are not dragging it across the biscuit - this way you will have a nice, even, smooth line.

4. When you want to finish, bring the bag down to the biscuit then stop squeezing and allow the nozzle to touch the biscuit at the finishing point to break contact.

CARAMEL GLUE / EDIBLE GLUE

Making caramel isn't for everyone. It can be tricky and during preparation this syrup becomes very hot, so be careful not to burn yourself. If possible, do this part without the kids, or alternatively, use the stiff peak icing on page 14 to stick your house together.

200g caster sugar
60ml cold water

TIP

Using a big frying pan for this makes it easy to dip the pieces of gingerbread into the pan to coat the edges.

1. Put the sugar and water in a large, low-sided frying pan. Place over a medium-high heat. Without stirring, bring to 160°C/320°F on a sugar thermometer. If you do not have one, you will know the syrup is ready when the sugar dissolves and turns a light golden colour.

2. Swirl the syrup gently in the pan to even out the colour. Then leave to cool for a few moments to thicken slightly to the consistency of honey.

3. If the syrup begins to harden in the pan, place it back over a gentle heat until it has returned to the required consistency.

BISCUITS

A range of biscuits to keep a variety
of abilities busy in the kitchen

FESTIVE HANGING BISCUITS

MAKES 40 - PREP: 45 MINUTES, PLUS COOLING - COOK: 20 MINUTES

Simply decorated festive biscuits add a touch of yum to your tree or home. Perfect for hanging just about anywhere, or to wrap up beautifully and give as a Christmas gift.

1 x quantity of Light or Dark Gingerbread Dough (see page 8)

TO DECORATE

1 x quantity of Royal Icing (see page 14)

red, white and silver sprinkles

YOU WILL NEED

Christmas cutters

string or ribbon

TIP

Have fun with the hanging materials – use twine, coloured ribbon or lace.

1. Heat the oven to 180°C/fan-assisted 160°C/gas mark 4. Line 2 large baking trays with silicone baking sheets or greaseproof paper.

2. Cut a large piece of greaseproof paper and roll out the gingerbread on top of it to 5mm. Using any Christmas themed cutter, cut out pieces of dough and use a palette knife to transfer them to the lined baking trays. Leave space for them to spread a little.

3. Using a straw, press one end into each of the biscuits where you would like to thread a ribbon to hang, twist the straw and pull away to remove a circle of dough. Or use a skewer to make a hole.

4. Place in the freezer for 5 minutes until hard. Bake in the oven in batches for 6–10 minutes depending on size, until golden brown at the edges. Check the hanging holes are still large enough to thread ribbon through; if not, use the straw or skewer again to increase the size. Leave to cool for 5 minutes on the trays then transfer to wire racks to cool completely.

5. Add a little water to the royal icing until you reach soft peak consistency. Spoon the icing into a piping bag fitted with a fine nozzle. Decorate the biscuits with dots, lines and swirls then add the sprinkles. Leave to cool completely for 4 hours before tying with ribbon and hanging.

GINGERBREAD FAMILY

MAKES 30 – PREP: 40 MINUTES, PLUS COOLING – COOK: 20 MINUTES

There is something very irresistible about gingerbread folk. Their wry little smiles and 'catch me if you can' demeanour brings a smile to your face whatever your age. Better still, they keep kids entertained for hours!

1 x quantity of Light Gingerbread Dough (see page 8). Halve the dough once made and add 40g of cocoa powder to one half

TO DECORATE

1 x quantity of Royal Icing (see page 14)

coloured chocolate beans

YOU WILL NEED

a set of gingerbread family cutters

1. Heat the oven to 160°C/fan-assisted 140°C/gas mark 3. Line 2 large baking trays with silicone baking sheets or greaseproof paper.

2. Cut a large piece of greaseproof paper and roll out one of the doughs on top of it to 5mm. Using gingerbread men, women and children cutters, cut out pieces of dough and use a palette knife to transfer them to the lined baking trays. Leave space for them to spread a little. Repeat with the second gingerbread dough.

3. Place in the freezer for 5 minutes until hard. Bake in the oven in batches for 6–10 minutes depending on size, until golden brown at the edges. Leave to cool for 5 minutes on the trays, then carefully transfer with a palette knife to wire racks to cool completely.

4. Add a little water to the royal icing until you reach a soft peak consistency. Spoon the icing into a piping bag fitted with a fine nozzle. Decorate the gingerbread people with the icing and coloured chocolate beans.

> **TIP** Dip some of the chocolate gingerbread figures in melted chocolate to create chocolate skirts or trousers!

SNOWFLAKE BISCUITS

MAKES 45 – PREP: 40 MINUTES, PLUS COOLING – COOK: 20 MINUTES

These sparkling snowflake biscuits are perfect for gift giving. Pop them in clear bags or little boxes for anyone who deserves a festive treat.

1 x quantity of Light or Dark Gingerbread Dough (see page 8)

TO DECORATE

2 x quantity of Royal Icing (see page 14)

1 large free-range egg white

50g granulated sugar

YOU WILL NEED

assorted snowflake cutters approx. 5cm, 7cm and 8cm

1. Heat the oven to 160°C/fan-assisted 140°C/gas mark 3. Line 2–3 large baking trays with silicone baking sheets or greaseproof paper.

2. Cut a large piece of greaseproof paper and roll out the gingerbread on top of it to 5mm. Using a range of snowflake cutters, cut out biscuits and place on the baking trays. Place larger biscuits on one baking sheet and smaller ones on the other so they bake at the same speed.

3. Bake in the oven in batches for 6–10 minutes depending on size, until golden brown at the edges. Leave to cool for 5 minutes on the trays then transfer to wire racks to cool completely.

4. Add a little water to the royal icing until you reach soft peak consistency. Spoon some of the icing into a piping bag fitted with a fine nozzle. In a steady and smooth line, pipe outlines around half of the snowflakes.

5. Add a little more water to the soft peak icing to make flood icing – a thick but runny consistency. Spoon into a piping bag, cut off the end and carefully fill the centres with icing. Sprinkle half the sugar over some of the biscuits while the icing is still wet.

6. Brush the remaining plain biscuits with the egg white and press into the sugar. Leave to set for 2 hours.

RUDOLPH BISCUITS

MAKES 40 – PREP: 1 HOUR 15 MINUTES, PLUS COOLING AND SETTING – COOK: 20 MINUTES

You start with a gingerbread man, turn him upside down and then you have Rudolph. It is simple and brilliant – the kids will go crazy for these!

1 x quantity of Dark Gingerbread Dough (see page 9)

TO DECORATE

3 x quantity of Royal Icing (see page 14)

red and black food colouring paste

60g cocoa powder

edible gold lustre powder

YOU WILL NEED

a gingerbread man cutter approx 9cm

1. Heat the oven to 160°C/fan-assisted 140°C/gas mark 3. Line 2 large baking trays with silicone baking sheets or greaseproof paper.

2. Cut a large piece of greaseproof paper and roll out the gingerbread on top of it to 5mm. Using a gingerbread man cutter, cut out pieces of dough and use a pallette knife to transfer them to the lined baking trays.

3. Place in the freezer for 5 minutes until hard. Bake in the oven in batches for 10 minutes until golden brown at the edges. Leave to cool for 5 minutes then carefully transfer with a palette knife to wire racks to cool completely.

4. Add a little water to the royal icing until you reach soft peak consistency. Get three small bowls and spoon 2 tablespoons of icing into each. Add red colouring to one, black to another and leave one white. Cover each with a damp cloth and then cover with cling film.

5. Add the cocoa powder to your remaining bowl of icing with a little water to bring it back to soft peak consistency and spoon into a piping bag fitted with a fine nozzle. Pipe outlines of Rudolph's head and antlers. Add a little extra water to the remaining brown icing to make flood icing – a thick but runny consistency. Spoon or pipe into the centres of the biscuits to fill the centres with icing. Leave to set for 4 hours or overnight.

6. For the red noses, repeat the process with the red icing, piping outlines, then filling with the flood icing. Use the white icing to pipe eyes. Leave to set for 15 minutes then pipe little black pupils and mouths with the black icing. Very carefully, using a paintbrush, dab the gold lustre powder and brush gently over the antlers. Leave to set completely for 1 hour.

GLASS-PRESSED
SANDWICH BISCUITS

MAKES 20 – PREP: 30 MINUTES – COOK: 20 MINUTES

This is an inventive way to transform a plain round biscuit into something elegant and worthy of serving to friends. It will also have you checking the bases of all your kitchenware!

1 x quantity of Light or Dark Gingerbread Dough (see page 8)

200g unsalted butter, softened

400g icing sugar, sifted

1 teaspoon vanilla extract

pinch of salt

YOU WILL NEED

assorted drinking glasses with embossed bases and a range of round cutters approx. 4cm–9cm

TIP

Experiment with anything that would leave a lovely pattern - like rolling the gingerbread dough over paper doilies. Just be sure to chill again before baking so the biscuits hold their shape.

1. Heat the oven to 160°C/fan-assisted 140°C/gas mark 3. Line 2 large baking trays with silicone baking sheets or greaseproof paper.

2. Cut a large piece of greaseproof paper and roll out the gingerbread on top of it to 5mm. Now select from your drinking glasses the ones that have the most beautiful patterns on their bases. Press one at a time into the dough firmly enough to leave an imprint but not so hard that you squash the whole biscuit! Then use a round biscuit cutter approx. 8cm to cut around the imprinted patterns. Use a range of sizes to make your collection of biscuits look more eclectic. Use a palette knife to transfer the biscuits onto the lined baking trays. Leave space for them to spread a little.

3. Place in the freezer for 5 minutes until hard - this second chill helps them to hold their shape and pattern better while baking. Bake in the oven in batches for 8–10 minutes until golden brown at the edges. Leave to cool for 5 minutes on the trays, then carefully transfer with a palette knife to wire racks to cool completely.

4. Beat the butter, icing sugar, vanilla and salt together with a handheld mixer until light and fluffy. Pipe or spread the butter icing onto the bases of half the biscuits and sandwich together with the remaining biscuits.

RUSSIAN DOLLS

MAKES 45 – PREP: 1 HOUR 30 MINUTES, PLUS COOLING AND SETTING – COOK: 20-30 MINUTES

Also known as matryoshka dolls, meaning 'little mother', as the dolls inside represent her children. Traditionally these wooden dolls are elaborately painted so I thought it was fitting to use a paint brush to decorate the biscuits.

1 x quantity of Light or Dark Gingerbread Dough (see page 8)

3 x quantity of Royal Icing (see page 14)

TO DECORATE

red, peach and black food colourings

YOU WILL NEED

Russian doll cutters approx. 6cm, 8cm and 10cm

a new fine paintbrush

1. Heat the oven to 160°C/fan-assisted 140°C/gas mark 3. Line 2 large baking trays with silicone baking sheets or greaseproof paper.

2. Cut a large piece of greaseproof paper and roll out the gingerbread on top of it to 5mm. Using Russian doll cutters, cut out pieces of dough and use a palette knife to transfer them to the lined baking trays.

3. Bake in the oven in batches for 6–10 minutes depending on size, until golden brown at the edges. Leave to cool for 5 minutes on the trays then transfer to wire racks to cool completely.

4. Add a little water to the royal icing until you reach soft peak consistency. Transfer 4 tablespoons to a small bowl, then cover the large bowl with a damp cloth and set aside. Add a little peach colouring to the icing and pipe small round circles for the doll faces. Add a little extra water to the remaining peach icing to make flood icing – a think but runny consistency. Spoon into the circles to fill the faces.

5. Transfer 2 tablespoons of the remaining white icing to a separate bowl, cover with a damp cloth and set aside. Add a little red food colouring to the large bowl of icing until you have a punchy red. With a fine nozzle, pipe a smooth red outline around the biscuits.

6. Add a little more water to the red icing to make flood icing, then use it to carefully fill the centres. Keep any remaining icing covered with a damp cloth. Leave to set completely for 4 hours or overnight.

7. Using a paintbrush and the reserved white icing, paint decorative patterns on the dolls' bodies and around the faces. Paint little red lips on the faces and tiny dots for nostrils. Use a drop of black colouring to paint eyes and eyelashes. Leave one final time to set for 2 hours.

TIP

Many snowman cutters have a very similar shape to a Russian doll, so check your cutter stash before buying a new one.

SPECULAAS

MAKES 12 LARGE BISCUITS - PREP: 40 MINUTES, PLUS CHILLING - COOK: 10-15 MINUTES

I grew up eating these, quite stale funnily enough, as they are baked in the Netherlands to celebrate Sinterklass/St. Nicolas Eve on the December 5th, but at Easter my sisters and I would visit my great Oma (Dutch for grandma) and she would give them to us!

100g butter, softened

150g soft light brown sugar

1 medium free-range egg

zest of 1 unwaxed lemon

200g plain flour, plus extra to dust the moulds

½ teaspoon baking powder

1 teaspoon ground cinnamon

1 teaspoon ground ginger

¼ teaspoon ground nutmeg

¼ teaspoon ground cloves

⅛ teaspoon ground white pepper

2 cardamom pods, husks removed and seeds ground

¼ teaspoon salt

50g ground almonds

30g flaked almonds

1 tablespoon milk

YOU WILL NEED

a speculaas plank - a wooden mould with an image or figure approx. 11cm x 7cm x 0.6cm. You can buy them in cookware shops, antique shops or online.

1. Put the butter and sugar in a large bowl and beat with an electric mixer until light and fluffy. Beat in the egg and lemon zest until well combined. Sift over the flour, baking powder, spices and salt and fold in with the ground almonds. Bring the dough together with your hands. Split into 2 balls, wrap in cling film and chill in the fridge for 1 hour.

2. Preheat the oven to 160°C/fan-assisted 140°C/gas mark 3. Line 2 large baking trays with silicone baking sheets or greaseproof paper. Take one half of the dough out of the fridge, keep the other dough chilled, because if it becomes sticky it is difficult to remove from the moulds.

3. Sprinkle a generous amount of flour into the speculaas plank, then brush excess gently out with a pastry brush. Take a small handful of dough and press into the mould. Use a sharp knife to cut away any excess. Press a few flaked almonds into the underside of the biscuits then tap gently out of the moulds. If they need a little help, run the tip of a knife around the edges. Check the mould frequently and clear away any dough left behind with a skewer.

4. Place on the lined baking trays and repeat with the remaining dough. Chill the biscuits in the freezer for 20 minutes. This second chill helps them to hold their shape better while baking.

5. Brush lightly with milk and bake in the oven for 10–15 minutes, until just golden brown at the edges. Leave to cool for 5 minutes on the trays, then transfer to wire racks to cool completely.

TIP If you do not have a speculaas plank, use a biscuit cutter or imprint with nice glass bases as on page 28.

GINGERBREAD SPICED
SPRINGERLE

MAKES 12 BISCUITS – PREP: 45 MINUTES, PLUS CHILLING AND SETTING – COOK: 10–15 MINUTES

Originating from Germany, these biscuits are made with hand-carved wooden moulds. You can pick up gorgeous moulds or rolling pins from antique stores. You can also use the imprinting method on page 33 used for the Speculaas biscuits.

¼ teaspoon baking powder

2 tablespoons milk

3 medium free-range eggs

375g icing sugar

75g unsalted butter, softened

zest of 1 unwaxed lemon

1 teaspoon ground ginger

½ teaspoon ground cinnamon

¼ teaspoon ground nutmeg

¼ teaspoon ground cloves

½ teaspoon salt

450g plain flour, plus extra for dusting

YOU WILL NEED

a Springerle mould, approx. 12cm diameter x 1.5cm deep

1. Line 2 large baking trays with silicone baking sheets or greaseproof paper. Stir the baking powder into 1 tablespoon of the milk and set aside for 30 minutes until dissolved.

2. Place the eggs in the bowl of a stand mixer and whisk on a high speed for 10 minutes until thick and pale. Slowly add the icing sugar, beating until creamy. Add the butter, zest, spices and salt and beat again until smooth and combined. Add the remaining milk and mix until just combined. On a slow speed, gradually add the flour in batches until the beater can't blend any more. Turn out onto a clean surface and knead in more flour to make a stiff dough. Wrap in cling film and chill in the fridge for 20 minutes.

3. Dust the surface with flour and roll out the gingerbread to 1cm. Sprinkle a generous amount of flour into the springerle mould. Gently brush excess out with a pastry brush. Imprint the dough with your mould, and cut around the mould with a sharp knife or use a biscuit cutter of a similar size. Press, cut and transfer to the lined baking sheets one at a time, so when you press the next one it does not distort the first. Leave to air-dry, uncovered, for 24 hours – this helps to preserve the detail of the surface pattern.

4. Heat the oven to 160°C/fan-assisted 140°C/gas mark 3. Lightly brush with the remaining milk and bake in the oven for 10–15 minutes depending on size, until lightly golden. Leave to cool for 5 minutes on the trays then transfer to wire racks to cool completely.

HOUSES

They look too good to eat,
but smell too good not to!

TOWN HOUSE

MAKES 1 HOUSE - PREP: 3 HOURS - COOK: 1 HOUR 15 MINUTES

This London town house will be your chic alternative to a traditional gingerbread house.

2 x quantity of Light or Dark Gingerbread Dough (see page 8)

1 x quantity of Caramel Glue (see page 16)

TO DECORATE

2 x quantity of Royal Icing (see page 14)

2-3 large sheets rice paper

YOU WILL NEED

the templates on page 96

TIP

You might find it easier to use some of the royal icing to help stick tricky bits together rather than using the glue.

1. See the templates on page 96. Using a ruler, cut out firm paper or card versions. Heat the oven to 160°C/fan-assisted 140°C/gas mark 3. Cut a large piece of greaseproof paper and roll out the gingerbread on top of it to 5mm. Using the templates cut out the pieces.

2. Transfer on the greaseproof paper to a baking tray. Place in the freezer for 10 minutes until hard. Bake in the oven in batches for 10-20 minutes, depending on size, until golden brown at the edges (see tip on page 48). Leave to cool for 5 minutes on the trays then transfer to wire racks to cool completely.

3. Add a little water to the royal icing until you reach soft peak consistency. Spoon into a piping bag fitted with a fine nozzle. Cut the rice paper 1-2cm larger than the grid of windows. Pipe around and between the windows on the underside of the gingerbread and stick the trimmed rice paper into place. Repeat for the roof windows. Pipe around the front door and attach the door piece so the door sits back from the front of the house. Pipe the window frames and panes.

4. Stick the lower fascia detail to the front and back using a little icing or glue. Then pipe around the outside of the lower third and around the windows. Save a little icing for sticking but add a little water to the remaining to make flood icing. Fill the piped areas until covered. Leave to set for 4 hours or overnight.

5. To assemble, dip one edge of the side wall into the caramel glue until the edge is covered. Attach to a front at a 90° angle and hold together while it hardens and sets. Continue by attaching another wall and then the back. Use a pastry brush to coat the top edges and attach the main roof. Stick on the remaining fascia details. Attach the roof windows to the walls, stick the top with the roof, then add the chimney pieces. Pipe 2 lines around the tops of the chimneys. Leave to set for 2 hours then place on the base of the house.

HOLLY ROOF HOUSE

MAKES 1 HOUSE · PREP: 2 HOURS, PLUS COOLING & SETTING · COOK: 1 HOUR

If you want a Christmas showstopper, look no further. Far from the overly decorated gingerbread houses full of sweets, this one is for the adults. It's glamorous and tempting – let's just hope you get to show it off before you break and eat it!

2 x quantity of Light or Dark Gingerbread Dough (see page 8)

1 x quantity of Caramel Glue (see page 16)

TO DECORATE

3 x quantity of Royal Icing (see page 14)

red and green food colouring paste

YOU WILL NEED

the templates on page 98

ribbon

1. See the templates on page 98. Using a ruler, cut out firm paper or card versions. Heat the oven to 160°C/fan-assisted 140°C/gas mark 3. Cut a large piece of greaseproof paper and roll out the gingerbread on top of it to 8mm. Using the templates cut out the house pieces. You can use any leftover dough to make gingerbread men.

2. Cut three thick slits on each of the roofs (see image on page 42) for the ribbon to hold the roof up. Transfer carefully on the greaseproof paper to a flat baking tray. Keep the dough on the greaseproof paper to prevent it from becoming misshapen while you move it. Place in the freezer for 10 minutes until hard then bake in the oven in batches for 10–20 minutes depending on size, until golden brown at the edges (see tip on page 48). Leave to cool for 5 minutes on the trays, then transfer to wire racks to cool completely.

3. To glue together, dip one edge of a front wall into the caramel glue until the edge is completely covered. Attach to a side wall at a 90° angle and hold together for a few moments while it hardens, then use tins or jars to support the walls while they set. Continue to stick together by attaching another wall and the back panel so you have the base of the gingerbread house. Leave to set completely for 1 hour or overnight. It needs to be firm to hold the weight of the roof.

4. Meanwhile, add a little water to the royal icing until you reach soft peak consistency. Spoon some of the icing into a piping bag fitted with a medium nozzle. Decorate by piping outlines of windows and doors etc.

5. Lay the roof pieces flat and in a steady and smooth line pipe outlines round the edges. Add a little extra water to two thirds of the soft peak icing to make flood icing – a thick but runny consistency. Spoon into a piping bag, cut off the end and carefully fill the centres with icing. Leave to set for 4 hours or overnight.

6. Once completely set, divide the remaining soft peak icing into two bowls and add a little red colouring paste to one and green to the other. Spoon into piping bags fitted with a fine nozzle to pipe holly leaves and berries and use a cocktail stick to drag out edges of the holly leaves. Add a little green icing or colouring paste to the leftover red icing to make it brown and pipe the holly tree branches. Carefully thread the roof panels with some ribbon and tie up together.

7. Remove the supports from the house and gently place the roof on the house.

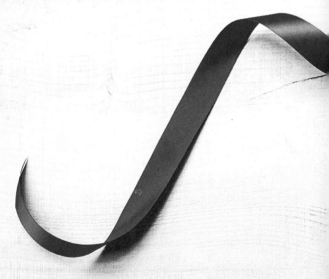

HANSEL & GRETEL HOUSE

MAKES 1 HOUSE - PREP: 2 HOURS, PLUS COOLING & SETTING - COOK: 1 HOUR

Gingerbread houses are intricately linked to the Brothers Grimm fairy tale of 'Hansel and Gretel' about a brother and sister who become lost in a forest and, when hungry and tired, they stumble across a house constructed of gingerbread and sweets! For most this would be a dream come true!

2 x quantity of Light or Dark Gingerbread Dough (see page 8)

1 x quantity of Caramel Glue (see page 16)

TO DECORATE

1 x quantity of Royal Icing (see page 14)

mini candy canes

lots of colourful sweets and chocolates

YOU WILL NEED

the templates on page 102

1. See the templates on page 102. Using a ruler, cut out firm paper or card versions. Heat the oven to 160°C/fan-assisted 140°C/gas mark 3. Cut a large piece of greaseproof paper and roll out the gingerbread on top of it to 8mm.

2. Using the templates, cut out the house pieces. Transfer carefully on the greaseproof paper to a flat baking tray. Keep the dough on the greaseproof paper to prevent it from becoming misshapen while you move it.

3. You can also cut a door or windows if you wish; it is best to do this once the dough is on the baking sheet – again this is to avoid misshaping it. Place in the freezer for 10 minutes until hard, then bake in the oven in batches for 10-20 minutes depending on size, until golden brown at the edges (see tip on page 48). Leave to cool for 5 minutes on the trays then transfer to wire racks to cool completely.

4. To glue together, dip one edge of a front wall into the caramel glue until the edge is completely covered. Attach to a side wall at a 90° angle and hold together for a few moments while it hardens and sets. Use tins or jars at first to support the walls while they set. Continue to stick together by attaching another wall and the back panel so you have the base of the gingerbread house. Leave to set completely for 30 minutes.

5. Remove the supports from the house and fix the roof panels on. You will need to reheat the caramel glue to return it to a liquid state. Use a pastry brush to coat the edges of the roof panels and edges of the base

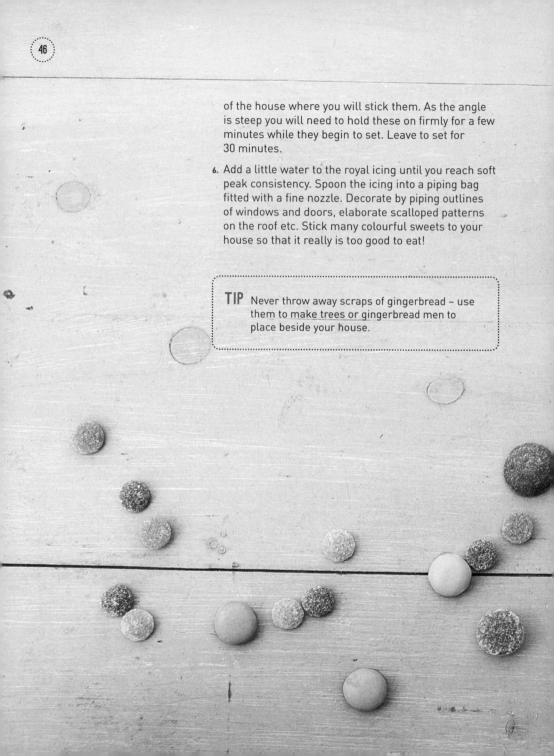

of the house where you will stick them. As the angle is steep you will need to hold these on firmly for a few minutes while they begin to set. Leave to set for 30 minutes.

6. Add a little water to the royal icing until you reach soft peak consistency. Spoon the icing into a piping bag fitted with a fine nozzle. Decorate by piping outlines of windows and doors, elaborate scalloped patterns on the roof etc. Stick many colourful sweets to your house so that it really is too good to eat!

> **TIP** Never throw away scraps of gingerbread – use them to make trees or gingerbread men to place beside your house.

GINGERBREAD STREET

MAKES 3 HOUSES - PREP: 2 HOURS, PLUS COOLING & SETTING - COOK: 1 HOUR

This street makes a lovely Christmas centrepiece when you cut out doors and windows and have candles or fairy lights twinkling around them.

2 x quantity of Light or Dark Gingerbread dough (see page 8)

TO DECORATE

3 x quantity of Royal Icing (see page 14)

liquorice wheel or edible sweet laces

1 x quantity of Caramel Glue (see page 16), optional

colourful chocolate beans or sweets

YOU WILL NEED

the templates on pages 99–101

TIP

Bake gingerbread for houses a little longer than individual biscuits as longer cooking times yield stiffer biscuits.

1. See the templates on pages 99–101. Using a ruler, cut out firm paper or card versions. Heat the oven to 160°C/fan-assisted 140°C/gas mark 3. Cut a large piece of greaseproof paper and roll out the gingerbread on top of it to 5mm.

2. Using the templates, cut out the house pieces and carefully transfer on the greaseproof paper (to prevent it from becoming misshapen while you move it) to a baking tray.

3. Place in the freezer for 5 minutes until hard, then bake in the oven in batches for 6–12 minutes depending on size, until golden brown at the edges. Leave to cool for 5 minutes, then transfer to wire racks to cool completely.

4. Add a little water to the royal icing until you reach soft peak consistency. Spoon one third of the icing into a piping bag fitted with a fine nozzle. To assemble the houses, pipe along the side edges of the wall pieces and stick to the front and back pieces. Pipe extra icing where the walls join each other on the inside of the house to create some support. Pipe icing onto the top edges of the side panels and front/back pieces where the roof pieces will be placed. Stick on the roofs and hold for a minute until the icing starts to set. Pipe decorations onto the houses.

5. Unroll the liquorice. Using icing or caramel glue, stick the colourful sweets to the liquorice and leave to set. Once set, stick to the front edge of the houses to look like festive street lights.

6. Add a little extra water to the remaining icing to make flood icing – a thick but runny consistency. Spoon over the peaks of the roofs and allow to drip down the sides. Leave to set for 2 hours or overnight.

COUNTRY COTTAGE

MAKES 1 HOUSE - PREP: 2 HOURS, PLUS COOLING & SETTING - COOK: 1 HOUR

An enchanting country cottage, complete with a porch and stained glass windows. Decorate simply with your favourite colours and interesting shapes!

2 x quantity of Light or Dark Gingerbread Dough (see page 8)

1 x quantity of Caramel Glue (see page 16)

TO DECORATE

2 x quantity of Royal Icing (see page 14)

200g yellow hard-boiled sweets

50g mints

YOU WILL NEED

the templates on pages 103–106

a 3.5cm heart cutter

1. See the templates on pages 103–106. Using a ruler, cut out firm paper or card versions. Heat the oven to 160°C/fan-assisted 140°C/gas mark 3. Cut a large piece of greaseproof paper and roll out the gingerbread on top of it to 5mm.

2. Using the templates cut out the house pieces, then cut out the door and windows. Carefully transfer on the greaseproof paper (to prevent it from becoming misshapen while you move it) to a flat baking tray.

3. Using a heart cutter, e.g. 3.5 cm, cut a window on the front panel of the porch and above the windows on the side panels. Crush half the boiled sweets to a powder. Pile high in the window and heart holes.

4. Add the hearts you have cut out to a baking tray. Place all the dough in the freezer for 10 minutes until hard, then bake in the oven in batches for 8–15 minutes depending on size, until golden brown at the edges (see tip on page 48). Leave to cool for 5 minutes on the trays then transfer to wire racks to cool completely.

5. To glue together, dip one edge of a front wall into the caramel glue until the edge is completely covered. Attach to a side wall at a 90° angle and hold together for a few moments while it hardens and sets. Continue to stick together by attaching another wall and the back panel so you have the base of the gingerbread house. Use tins or jars to support the walls while they set. Stick the porch base together and stick to the house. Leave to set completely for 30 minutes.

6. Remove the supports from the house and fix the roof panels on using a pastry brush to coat the edges of the roof panels and edges of the base of the house where you will stick them. Then attach the roof panels to the porch. Use the caramel glue to stick the chimney pieces together. Once hard, glue to the roof.

7. Add a little water to the royal icing until you reach soft peak consistency. Spoon some of the icing into a piping bag fitted with a fine nozzle. Decorate by piping scalloped lines onto the roof for a tiled roof, snow onto the window frames and outline the door. Finish by using the soft peak icing to stick coloured sweets to your house.

CREATIONS

From a chocolate bird house to a hanging
wreath, there are plenty of ideas here
to inspire your next edible project

EDIBLE STAR WREATH

MAKES 1 WREATH ~ PREP: 2 HOURS, PLUS CHILLING & SETTING ~ COOK: 45 MINUTES

Bake this pretty wreath to hang on your door or serve it as a fun, sharing dessert!

···

2 x quantity of Light or
Dark Gingerbread Dough
(see page 8)

2 x quantity of
Royal Icing
(see page 14)

1 x quantity of Caramel
Glue (see page 16)

TO DECORATE

blue food
colouring paste

10g silver balls

YOU WILL NEED

star cutters
approx. 3cm, 5cm
and 7cm

1. Heat the oven to 160°C/fan-assisted 140°C/gas mark 3.
   Line 3 large baking trays with silicone baking sheets or
   greaseproof paper.

2. Cut a large piece of greaseproof paper and roll out the
   gingerbread on top of it to 5mm. Place a 25cm plate on the
   dough and cut round it. Then use a smaller plate or bowl to
   cut out the centre – you want a ring 4cm wide.

3. Using different-sized star cutters, cut out shapes from the
   remaining dough. You will need about 30 biscuits. Place
   in the freezer for 5 minutes until hard. Bake in the oven in
   batches for 6–15 minutes depending on size, until golden
   brown at the edges. Bake the wreath ring for 15 minutes or
   until golden as it will need to be sturdy. Leave to cool for 5
   minutes on the trays, then carefully transfer with a palette
   knife to wire racks to cool completely.

4. Add a little water to the royal icing until you reach soft peak
   consistency. Divide between 2 bowls and colour one with
   blue colouring paste. Spoon each into piping bags fitted
   with fine nozzles. Pipe outlines around half the snowflakes.
   Pipe decorations onto the plain stars.

5. Squeeze two thirds of the icing out of the piping bags into
   separate bowls and add water to make flood icing – a thick
   but runny consistency. Spoon into the biscuits lined with
   the same colour. Stud a few with silver balls. Leave to set for
   2 hours, then use the remaining soft peak icing to pipe more
   detail onto the stars.

6. Arrange the largest stars on the ring. Once you are happy
   with the placing, brush the backs of the stars
   with caramel glue and stick to the circle. Repeat with
   the remaining stars. Leave to set. Hang with a ribbon.

MINI MUG GINGERBREAD HOUSES

MAKES 15 HOUSES - PREP: 1 HOUR 30 MINUTES, PLUS CHILLING & COOLING - COOK: 20 MINUTES

These mini houses sit happily on the edge of your mug and go perfectly with an afternoon cup of tea. Or try them with a gingerbread latte using the syrup on page 94.

1 x quantity of Light Gingerbread Dough (see page 8)

TO DECORATE

2 x quantity of Royal Icing (see page 14)

icing sugar, to dust

white sprinkles and snowflakes

YOU WILL NEED

the templates on page 107

TIP

Check the thickness of your mugs. Usually they are 3mm, but if you think yours are thicker, make the door opening a little wider.

1. Heat the oven to 160°C/fan-assisted 140°C/gas mark 3. Line 2 or 3 large baking trays with silicone baking sheets or greaseproof paper. See the templates on page 107. Using a ruler, cut out firm paper or card versions.

2. Cut a large piece of greaseproof paper and roll out the gingerbread on top of it to 5mm. Using the templates cut out the house pieces. Place on a lined baking tray. Repeat to make 14 more houses.

3. Place in the freezer for 5 minutes until hard. Bake in the oven for 5–6 minutes or until golden brown at the edges. Use the flat edge of a sharp knife to straighten any edges that have spread during baking, especially the doorway so it will fit over the rim of your mugs. Leave to cool for 5 minutes on the trays, then transfer with a palette knife to wire racks to cool.

4. Add a little water to the royal icing until you reach soft peak consistency. Spoon some of the icing into a piping bag fitted with a fine nozzle. Pipe along the side edges of the wall pieces and stick to the door pieces. Pipe extra icing where the walls join each other on the inside of the house to create some support.

5. Pipe icing onto the top edges of the side panels and front/back pieces where the roof pieces will be placed. Stick on the roofs and hold for a minute until the icing starts to set. Then stick on the chimneys.

6. Use the remaining icing to decorate. Cover some of the roofs with icing and sprinkle over decorations. Use a cocktail stick to help create icicles. Leave to set for 2 hours or overnight.

CHRISTMAS BISCUIT TREE

MAKES 1 LARGE TREE - PREP: 1 HOUR 30 MINUTES, PLUS CHILLING & SETTING - COOK: 1 HOUR

This biscuit tree is so simple yet it looks so impressive (even if the kids help to make it!). A little dusting of icing sugar or sprinkles add to the magic.

1 x quantity of Light or Dark Gingerbread Dough (see page 8)

TO DECORATE

2 x quantity of Royal Icing (see page 14)

2 tablespoons icing sugar

sprinkles, optional

1. Heat the oven to 160°C/fan-assisted 140°C/gas mark 3. Line 2 or 3 large baking trays with silicone baking sheets or greaseproof paper. Using a ruler, draw and cut out a 20cm star onto firm paper or card. Then inside this star draw smaller stars decreasing by 2cm each time, your last star being 2cm.

2. Cut a large piece of greaseproof paper and roll out the gingerbread on top of it to 5mm. Cut out three of the largest stars and using a palette knife transfer to the lined baking sheets. Place in the freezer for 5 minutes until hard then bake in the oven in batches for 6–10 minutes depending on size, until golden brown at the edges. Leave to cool for 5 minutes on the trays, then carefully transfer with a palette knife to wire racks to cool completely.

3. Trim the star template to the next size and cut out three dough stars, chill and bake as above decreasing the bake time to 6–8 minutes for medium stars and to 3–6 minutes for the small stars. Keep repeating until you have baked three of each star.

4. Add a little water to the royal icing until you reach soft peak consistency. Spoon into a piping bag fitted with a medium round nozzle and pipe around each of the stars. Add a little more water to the remaining icing to make flood icing, and spoon or pipe into the lines of each biscuit spreading to the edges. Leave for 30 minutes to set, then stack the stars up starting with the largest and ending with the smallest on its edge. Dust with the icing sugar and decorate with sprinkles if you wish.

TIP

I like to make one giant tree that slowly gets devoured, but you could make a few smaller trees to display together or enjoy at different times.

CHOCOLATE BIRD HOUSE

MAKES 1 HOUSE PLUS 20 BIRDS - PREP: 2 HOURS, PLUS COOLING & SETTING - COOK: 1 HOUR

For the more whimsical among you, this is the perfect project. It is also a great excuse to make a gingerbread house at any time of the year!

1 x quantity of Dark Gingerbread Dough (see page 9). Add 60g of cocoa to the dough to make it chocolate flavoured

1 x quantity of Caramel Glue (see page 16)

TO DECORATE

2 x quantity of Royal Icing (see page 14)

blue, yellow and black food colouring paste

150g dark chocolate, melted

250g large chocolate buttons

100g chocolate Matchmakers/sticks

YOU WILL NEED

the templates on page 108

1. See the templates on page 108. Using a ruler, cut out firm paper or card versions. Heat the oven to 160°C/ fan-assisted 140°C/gas mark 3. Cut a large piece of greaseproof paper and roll out the gingerbread on top of it to 5mm. Using the templates, cut out the house pieces.

2. Transfer carefully on the greaseproof paper (to prevent it from becoming misshapen while you move it) to a flat baking tray. Place in the freezer for 5 minutes until hard, then bake in the oven in batches for 10–15 minutes depending on size, until golden brown at the edges. Leave to cool for 5 minutes on the trays then transfer to wire racks to cool completely.

3. Using bird cutters, cut out pieces from the remaining dough and bake for 8 minutes. Leave to cool for 5 minutes on the trays then transfer to wire racks to cool completely.

4. To assemble the house, dip one edge of the front wall into the caramel glue until the edge is completely covered. Attach to a side wall at a 90° angle and hold together for a few moments while it hardens and sets. Continue to stick together by attaching another wall and the back panel so you have the base of the bird house. To fix the roof panels on, you may need to reheat the caramel glue to return it to a liquid state. Use a pastry brush to coat the edges of the roof panels and edges of the base of the house where you will stick them. Hold these on firmly for a few minutes while they begin to set. Leave to set for 30 minutes.

5. Meanwhile, add a little water to the royal icing until you reach soft peak consistency. Spoon one third into a bowl, cover with a damp cloth and set aside. In the large bowl of icing, stir through a little blue colouring paste, spoon half into a piping bag fitted with a fine nozzle and pipe an outline around the birds. Add a little extra water to the remaining blue icing to make flood icing – a thick but runny consistency. Spoon or pipe into the centres of the biscuits. Leave to completely set, about 2 hours.

6. Add yellow food colouring to the reserved icing and use to pipe wing details and beaks. Use a paintbrush and black colouring mixed with a drop of water to draw eyes and feet. Leave to set for 1 hour.

7. Sit the bird house on the round base. Brush the bottom 3cm of the roof with melted chocolate and cover with a row of chocolate buttons. Repeat brushing and sticking rows up the roof to the top. Repeat the process with the front but with chocolate sticks, breaking pieces to fit flush with the edges.

8. Use a small blob of chocolate to stick a couple of birds in place. I like to keep the remaining bird biscuits stacked up in the bird house!

GINGERBREAD GARLAND

MAKES 4 GARLANDS - PREP: 40 MINUTES - COOK: 20 MINUTES

This adorable gingerbread garland is a great activity for the kids in the run up to Christmas. Just make sure you hang it out of the reach of young children or pets... or the biscuits will be enjoyed before you get a chance!

1 x quantity of Light Gingerbread Dough (see page 8). Halve the dough once made and add 40g of cocoa powder to one half

YOU WILL NEED
gingerbread man and heart cutters approx. 6cm

4 x 1 meter lengths of ribbon

1. Heat the oven to 160°C/fan-assisted 140°C/gas mark 3. Line 2 large baking trays with silicone baking sheets or greaseproof paper. Cut a large piece of greaseproof paper and roll out the gingerbread on top of it to 5mm.

2. Using a gingerbread man and heart cutter, cut out pieces of dough and use a palette knife to transfer them to the lined baking trays. Leave space for them to spread a little. Repeat with the other dough. Place in the freezer for 5 minutes until hard.

3. Cut two slits in the centre of each biscuit 1cm apart, large enough to thread a ribbon through. Bake in the oven in batches for 12 minutes, until golden brown at the edges. Check the slits are still large enough, if not cut back to size. Leave to cool for 5 minutes on the trays then carefully transfer with a palette knife to wire racks to cool completely.

4. Thread the biscuits onto a long piece of ribbon, always starting at the back of the biscuit going through to the front, then turning and threading back through to the back. This ensures that the length of the ribbon always stays at the back of the garland, so it doesn't cover the biscuits. Don't pull the ribbon too tight when hanging or the pressure will break the centre of the biscuits.

TIP

Hang against a flat surface to prevent the weight rolling the biscuits forward.

WILDLIFE WONDERLAND

MAKES 1 LARGE TREE & 20 ASSORTED ANIMALS - PREP: 1 HOUR, PLUS 30 MINUTES CHILLING - COOK: 50 MINUTES

Bring your biscuits to life by adding a little stand and surrounding them with edible earth and trees!

2 x quantity of Light or Dark Gingerbread Dough (see page 8)

1 x quantity of Caramel Glue (see page 16)

TO DECORATE

200g white chocolate, melted

50g mixed green and white sprinkles

2 x quantity of Royal Icing (see page 14)

60g cocoa powder

300g biscuit crumbs

1. Heat the oven to 160°C/fan-assisted 140°C/gas mark 3. Line 2 or 3 large baking trays with silicone baking sheets or greaseproof paper. Cut a large piece of greaseproof paper and roll out the gingerbread on top of it to 5mm.

2. Using any wildlife themed cutter, cut out pieces of dough and use a palette knife to transfer them to lined baking trays. Leave space for them to spread a little. If you want to stand your biscuits, use a small round biscuit cutter to cut pieces of dough large enough to stand your wildlife biscuits on. Place in the freezer for 5 minutes until hard then bake in the oven in batches for 6–10 minutes depending on size, until golden brown at the edges. Leave to cool for 5 minutes on the trays then carefully transfer with a palette knife to wire racks to cool completely.

3. Make a large 3D tree following the method on page 72 for the 3D Christmas tree biscuits. But instead of making lots of little trees, make one large one. If you do not have a large cutter, make a template for a large tree out of card. Chill, bake and cool as above.

4. Once cool, use a pastry brush to brush the white chocolate down the edges of the tree and scatter over or press into the sprinkles. Leave to set before slotting the three biscuits into each other.

5. Add a little water to the royal icing until you reach soft peak consistency. Spoon half into a piping bag fitted with a small round nozzle. Stir the cocoa powder into the remaining icing, adding a little water to return it to

peak. Spoon into a separate piping bag fitted with a small round nozzle. Use both icings to pipe details onto the animals. Leave to set completely for 2 hours.

6. Spoon a little caramel glue onto the biscuit bases, place the animal biscuits on the glue and hold for a moment while they begin to set. Scatter the biscuit crumbs over a board and arrange the wildlife around the tree.

3D CHRISTMAS TREE

MAKES 18 - PREP: 2 HOURS, PLUS COOLING & SETTING - COOK: 20-30 MINUTES

These fun trees stand up by themselves and make for a much more exciting Christmas tree biscuit! You can use this recipe to make small trees for individual servings, large trees for sharing or to display beside a gingerbread house.

1 x quantity of Light or Dark Gingerbread Dough (see page 8)

TO DECORATE

200g white chocolate, melted
50g mixed green and white sprinkles

YOU WILL NEED

a tree cutter approx. 9cm

the template on page 109

1. Take your tree cutter and trace three times onto a thick card. Using a ruler, draw a vertical line straight down the centre of the trees. Draw two more lines 1cm either side of your first line. Cut around the trees cutting off the tree trunk to make it more stable.

2. Refer to page 109 for how to cut your tree templates. Measure from the top of the tree to the bottom and divide by three. Double this measurement, add 5mm and mark on your first tree measuring from the bottom up. For the second tree, use your original measurement add 5mm and mark from the top down and then the bottom up. For the third, double the original measurement add 5mm and measure from the top down. Cut down the two widest lines to your marks and remove to create slots.

3. Heat the oven to 160°C/fan-assisted 140°C/gas mark 3. Line 2 large baking trays with silicone baking sheets or greaseproof paper. Cut a large piece of greaseproof paper and roll out the gingerbread on top of it to 5mm.

4. Using your tree cutter, cut out pieces of dough three at a time for each biscuit. Transfer to the lined baking trays. Using the templates and a sharp knife, cut out the slots and remove the trunk from each biscuit. Repeat with the remaining dough.

5. Place in the freezer for 5 minutes until hard. Bake in the oven in batches for 8–10 minutes, until golden at the edges. Leave to cool for 5 minutes, then transfer with a palette knife to wire racks to cool completely.

6. Using a pastry brush, brush the white chocolate down the edges of the trees and scatter over the sprinkles. Leave to set before slotting the 3 biscuits into each other.

BAKES

For when you crave something
a little softer and stickier

GINGERBREAD LAYER CAKE
WITH MAPLE ICING

SERVES: 12 - PREP: 40 MINUTES - COOK: 30-35 MINUTES

A great alternative to Christmas cake with a rich and sticky sponge and a tangy cream cheese icing. Decorate with Mini Gingerbread Houses for a show stopper!

100g dark molasses/ black treacle

100g golden syrup/honey

250g light brown muscovado sugar

250g softened butter

3 medium free-range eggs

250ml milk

350g plain flour

1½ teaspoons bicarbonate of soda

2 teaspoons ground ginger

1 teaspoon cinnamon

1 teaspoon allspice

¼ teaspoon nutmeg

½ teaspoon salt

zest of 1 unwaxed lemon

TO DECORATE

250g butter, softened

500g icing sugar

250g full fat cream cheese at room temperature

2 tablespoons maple syrup

3 tablespoons desiccated coconut

2 x Mini Gingerbread Mug Houses (see page 60)

YOU WILL NEED

3 x 18cm round cake tins

1. Heat the oven to 180°C/fan-assisted 160°C/gas mark 4. Grease and line the cake tins with greaseproof paper.

2. Pour the molasses, syrup, sugar and butter into a large saucepan and melt over a low/medium heat, stirring frequently until the sugar has dissolved. Pour into the bowl of a stand mixer or a large bowl and leave to cool for 10 minutes.

3. Beat the eggs and milk together then beat into the cooled treacle mixture with a handheld or stand mixer. Sift the remaining dry ingredients over the wet mix and beat in with the lemon zest until just combined.

4. Divide the batter evenly between the lined tins. Bake in the oven for 20–25 minutes, until risen and a skewer emerges clean. Leave to cool for 10 minutes in the tins then transfer to wire racks to cool completely.

5. Using a stand mixer or electric hand mixer, beat the butter and icing sugar together until pale and fluffy. Add the cream cheese and continue to beat for another 2 minutes until smooth, then beat in the maple syrup for a further 30 seconds.

6. Spread a little icing over the first layer of sponge then top with the next layer of sponge. Repeat once more then use the remaining icing to top the cake and cover the sides. Sprinkle over the coconut and top with Mini Gingerbread Houses.

GINGERBREAD CUPCAKES
WITH CHOCOLATE ICING

MAKES 12 – PREP:40 MINUTES, PLUS COOLING – COOK: 30 MINUTES

Sticky dark English gingerbread cupcakes smothered in chocolate buttercream. Use up leftover gingerbread dough to make mini gingerbread man biscuits to decorate.

150g unsalted butter, softened

225g dark muscovado sugar

150g dark molasses/black treacle

zest of 1 unwaxed orange

1 teaspoon ground cinnamon

1 teaspoon ground ginger

½ teaspoon ground nutmeg

¼ teaspoon ground allspice

3 medium free-range eggs

100g apple sauce

150g plain flour

½ teaspoon baking powder

½ teaspoon bicarbonate of soda

¼ teaspoon salt

ICING AND DECORATION

250g butter, softened

250g icing sugar, sifted

100g dark chocolate, melted and cooled

30g crystallised ginger or mini gingerbread men (see page 22)

1. Heat the oven to 180°C/fan-assisted160°C/gas mark 4. Line a 12-hole muffin tray with cupcake cases.

2. Put the butter, sugar, molasses, zest and spices in a medium saucepan and melt over a low/medium heat. Stir frequently until the sugar has dissolved. Pour into the bowl of a stand mixer or a large bowl and leave to cool for 10 minutes.

3. Add the eggs one at a time, beating well with a handheld or stand mixer after each addition. Beat in the apple sauce. Sift over the dry ingredients then mix on a slow speed until just combined.

4. Spoon the mixture into the cupcake cases. Use a large ice cream scoop to make the cakes even sizes. Bake in the oven for 20 minutes, until risen and a skewer emerges clean. Leave to cool for 10 minutes in the muffin tray, then transfer to wire racks to cool completely.

5. Beat the butter and icing sugar together with a handheld mixer until light and fluffy. Add the cooled chocolate and beat until smooth and combined. Spoon into a piping bag fitted with a large open star nozzle.

6. Hold the bag vertically and pipe in a spiral pattern working from the outside edge inward keeping a constant pressure on the icing bag. Continue in a spiral motion creating another layer of icing working gradually toward the centre. To finish, release the pressure on the bag, press down lightly then draw up sharply. Decorate with the crystallised ginger or mini gingerbread men.

ICING VARIATIONS:

Cream cheese – ½ quantity cream cheese icing from Gingerbread Layer Cake (see page 76)

Orange – Scatter with orange zest or add a little orange juice to the buttercream

Vanilla – Omit the chocolate and add a teaspoon of vanilla extract to the buttercream

Spiced – Add a pinch of ground ginger or cinnamon to the buttercream

PAIN D'EPICES
WITH CHOCOLATE SAUCE

SERVES 12 – PREP: 20 MINUTES, PLUS COOLING – COOK: 45 MINUTES

This is my take on the French classic 'spice bread'. Delicious on its own or spread with a little butter, but best served my way with a glossy chocolate orange sauce!

300g runny clear honey

200g dark soft brown sugar

100g unsalted butter, plus extra for greasing

400g plain flour

1 teaspoon baking powder

1 teaspoon bicarbonate of soda

½ teaspoon salt

2 teaspoons ground ginger

1 teaspoon ground cinnamon

1 teaspoon ground nutmeg

½ teaspoon ground cloves

60g ground almonds

zest of 1 unwaxed lemon

3 medium free-range eggs

50ml dark rum

1 teaspoon almond extract

FOR THE CHOCOLATE SAUCE

125ml double cream

1 tablespoon dark soft brown sugar

25g unsalted butter

1 tablespoon golden syrup

75g dark chocolate (70% cocoa), finely chopped

1 tablespoon Cointreau

1. Put the honey, sugar and butter in a medium saucepan and place over a low heat. Melt together stirring frequently until the sugar has dissolved. Leave to cool for 15 minutes.

2. Heat the oven to 180°C/fan-assisted 160°C/gas mark 4. Generously grease a 2-litre (20 x 10cm) Bundt tin or a 20cm round deep cake tin.

3. Sieve the flour, baking powder, bicarbonate of soda, salt and spices into a large bowl. Fold through the ground almonds and lemon zest.

4. Pour the melted honey mixture into the flour mix and using an electric whisk beat together. Add the eggs, rum and almond extract and beat together until combined.

5. Pour into the greased tin and bake on the middle shelf of the oven for 25 minutes before covering with a double layer of foil. Return to the oven for a further 15 minutes or until a skewer emerges clean. Leave to cool for 15 minutes in the tin then turn out onto a wire rack to cool completely.

6. To make the chocolate sauce, put the cream, sugar, butter and golden syrup in a small saucepan. Place over a low/medium heat and stir until the sugar dissolves. Remove from the heat and stir through the chopped chocolate until melted and glossy. Finally add the Cointreau and gently stir until combined.

7. Drizzle the hot sauce over the cake or serve separately.

APPLE & GINGERBREAD STREUSEL TART

MAKES 1 TART - PREP: 30 MINUTES, PLUS CHILLING - COOK: 40 MINUTES

The use of gingerbread in place of pastry in this happy blend of English apple crumble, Dutch apple pie and German streusel makes it unlike other tarts you have had before.

½ x quantity of Dark Gingerbread Dough (see page 9)

FOR THE FILLING

2 (approx. 360g) Bramley apples, peeled and cored

3 (approx. 300g) medium eating apples, peeled and cored

juice of 1 unwaxed lemon

75g granulated sugar

75g soft light brown sugar

3 tablespoons plain flour

1 teaspoon ground cinnamon

¼ teaspoon ground allspice

½ teaspoon salt

75g sultanas

20g butter, cubed

FOR THE STREUSEL TOPPING

40g plain flour

40g granulated sugar

½ teaspoon ground ginger

pinch of salt

60g cold butter, cut into small cubes

30g pecans, roughly chopped

1. Heat the oven to 180°C/fan-assisted 160°C/gas mark 4. Cut a large piece of greaseproof paper and roll out the gingerbread on top of it to 5mm thick x 32cm diameter. Line a deep 23cm fluted pie dish with the dough. Press gently into the edges and trim any excess with a sharp knife. Reserve the trimmings. Place the tart case in the freezer to chill for 20 minutes.

2. Meanwhile cut the apples into 5mm thick slices, squeeze over the lemon juice, then toss in a large bowl with the sugars, flour, spices, salt and sultanas.

3. Pile high into the chilled gingerbread case, then press down to fill the gaps. Dot with the butter and place on a baking tray to catch any spills. Bake for 20 minutes on the middle shelf of the oven.

4. To make the streusel, mix the flour, sugar, ginger and salt until combined. Cut 50g of the reserved gingerbread dough into small chunks and add to the mix with the butter. Rub together with the tips of your fingers to form clumps. Stir through the pecans.

5. After the tart has baked for 20 minutes, sprinkle over the streusel and return to the oven to bake for a further 30 minutes, or until the tart is golden and bubbling and the apples are tender when pierced with a sharp knife. Remove from the oven and set aside to cool slightly before serving. Alternatively, serve chilled.

GINGERBREAD KNOTS

MAKES: 12 – PREP:45 MINUTES, PLUS COOLING & RISING – COOK: 20 MINUTES

This is a twist on the Swedish cinnamon buns that are scattered with crunchy pearl sugar. It's easy to make these look great – just twist up the dough and you're done!

300ml whole milk

6 cardamom pods, husks removed and seeds ground

50g butter

450g strong white flour

1 tablespoon ground ginger

7g fast action yeast

50g caster sugar

½ teaspoon salt

2 medium free-range eggs

1 tablespoon olive oil

4 tablespoons pearl sugar or sugar nibs (large grains of pure sugar that don't melt in the oven)

FOR THE GINGERBREAD FILLING

100g salted butter, softened

80g soft dark brown sugar

zest of ½ unwaxed orange

2 teaspoons ground ginger

1 teaspoon ground cinnamon

½ teaspoon ground nutmeg

¼ teaspoon ground cloves

½ teaspoon salt

1. Place the milk and ground cardamom seeds in a small saucepan and bring just to the boil. Remove from the heat and stir in the butter until melted. Set aside to reduce in temperature to lukewarm.

2. Meanwhile sift the flour, ginger, yeast, caster sugar and salt into a bowl. Make a well in the centre and mix in 1 egg. Once the milk is lukewarm, pour over the dry mixture and stir until it comes together to make a soft, sticky dough.

3. Knead for 10 minutes using an electric dough hook until it is smooth and springs back a little. If kneading by hand, tip out onto an oiled surface and knead for 10 minutes. The dough will be very sticky to begin with but do not add any additional flour. Transfer to a clean bowl greased with oil. Cover loosely with greased cling film and leave in a warm place for 30 minutes until it has nearly doubled in size.

4. To make the filling, beat the butter, sugar, zest, spices and salt together until soft and spreadable. Set aside.

5. Lightly flour a clean surface and dust your hands in flour. Tip out the dough, turn once to lightly coat in the flour and divide it in half. Roll one piece into a large rectangle, about 40cm x 50cm. Spread half of the filling on top.

6. Fold one third of the dough over the second third. Then take the third piece and fold over the first and second piece. You will now have three layers of dough that look like how you would fold a letter. Cut the dough into 6 long strips approximately 2cm wide. Twist each strip together into a knot, tucking any ends underneath and place evenly spread on a large baking tray lined with a silicone baking sheet or greaseproof paper. Repeat with the remaining dough

and gingerbread filling and place on a second lined baking tray.

7. Cover loosely with greased cling film and leave once again in a warm place for 30 minutes until nearly doubled in size. Heat the oven to 200°C/fan-assisted 180°C/gas mark 6. Brush very lightly with beaten egg and sprinkle with pearl sugar. Bake in the oven for 8-10 minutes, until lightly golden brown.

VARIATIONS

Chocoholic – Add 1 tablespoon of cocoa powder to the filling or 2 tablespoons to the dough! Yum!

Go nutty – Sprinkle 50g finely chopped pecans or hazelnuts over the filling before folding.

TIP For a consistent warm place to rise dough, place a bowl of boiling water in the base of a cold oven and place the dough bowl covered in cling film at the top.

LEBKUCHEN

MAKES 24 – PREP: 45 MINUTES, PLUS COOLING & SETTING – COOK: 20 MINUTES

Lebkuchen is a German gingerbread that has become synonymous with Christmas baking. A cross between a biscuit and cake with a delicious mixture of honey, almond, ginger and cocoa, it is another front runner for edible gifts.

160g runny clear honey

110g unsalted butter

50g ground almonds

250g plain flour

½ teaspoon baking powder

¾ teaspoon bicarbonate of soda

1 tablespoon ground ginger

2 teaspoons ground cinnamon

½ teaspoon ground nutmeg

¼ teaspoon ground cloves

2 teaspoons cocoa powder

¼ teaspoon salt

TO DECORATE

150g icing sugar

1 medium egg white

2–3 tablespoons cold water

100g dark chocolate, melted

YOU WILL NEED

a 4cm heart cutter

1. Melt the honey and butter in a small saucepan over a low heat. Stir occasionally until combined. Remove from the heat and set aside to cool for 15 minutes.

2. Heat the oven to 160°C/fan-assisted 140°C/gas mark 3. Line 2 large baking trays with silicone baking sheets or greaseproof paper.

3. Place the ground almonds in a large bowl and sieve over the remaining ingredients. Pour over the cooled honey mixture and stir until it comes together to make a dough.

4. Divide the dough and set one half aside. Roll the other half into small equal balls, place on a lined baking sheet and press each one down slightly with the palm of your hand to approx. 2cm thick.

5. Roll out the remaining dough to 2cm thick and, using a 4cm heart cutter, cut into biscuits. Soften the edges of the hearts with your fingers. Place on the other lined baking sheet. Bake in the oven for 8–10 minutes, until just golden brown at the edges. Leave to cool for 5 minutes on the trays then transfer to wire racks to cool completely.

6. Meanwhile, mix the icing sugar, egg white and water together to make a thin runny icing. Place a baking sheet under the wire rack and thinly brush the lebkuchen with the icing using a pastry brush. Leave for 15 minutes to set, then repeat with the remaining icing. Leave to set.

7. Dip half of the lebkuchen into the melted chocolate to coat the base and a few millimetres up the side. Then drizzle the remaining half with a zig-zag of chocolate.

TIP These biscuits really do improve with age, that's if you can bear to wait and you must!

INGREDIENTS IN A JAR GIFT
CHEWY GINGERBREAD COOKIES

MAKES 1 LITRE JAR/ 22 BISCUITS - PREP: 15 MINUTES, PLUS CHILLING - COOK: 10 MINUTES

This is such a fun gift to give friends. You can mix up the spices, chocolate chips and crystallised ginger to make different flavoured cookies.

200g plain flour

1 teaspoon baking power

1 teaspoon bicarbonate of soda

½ teaspoon salt

100g dark brown sugar

2 teaspoons ground ginger

1 teaspoon ground cinnamon

½ teaspoon ground nutmeg

¼ teaspoon ground cloves

125g rolled oats

100g white chocolate chips

100g crystallised ginger, finely chopped

YOU WILL NEED

a 1 litre jar

IF MAKING THE COOKIES YOURSELF YOU WILL ALSO NEED

110g unsalted butter

100g dark molasses/ black treacle

75g golden syrup/honey

1 medium free-range egg, lightly beaten

To make a layered jar:

1. Pack each layer down tightly into the jar pressing with your fist or the back of a spoon. You will need to pack it in well or the ingredients will not fit. Leave a few oats out if there isn't space.

First - flour, baking powder, bicarbonate of soda and salt
Second - dark brown sugar
Third - spices
Fourth - oats
Fifth - chocolate chips
Sixth - crystallised ginger

2. Make a label giving the following instructions:

You will need: 110g unsalted butter, 100g black treacle, 75g golden syrup and 1 medium egg

In a large saucepan melt the butter, treacle and golden syrup together until combined. Leave to cool for 5 minutes, then tip the contents of the jar into the saucepan and mix together until combined.

Roll the dough into 4cm balls and place on lined baking trays approx. 4cm apart. Chill in the fridge for 20 minutes.

Heat the oven to 180°C/fan-assisted 160°C/gas mark 4. Bake for 10 minutes, until the surface has cracked. Leave to cool for 5 minutes on the trays, then transfer to wire racks to cool completely.

If you are making the cookies yourself, use the fresh ingredients listed and follow the same directions you would write on a label!

GINGERBREAD SYRUP

MAKES 300ML - PREP: 10 MINUTES, PLUS COOLING - COOK: 20-25 MINUTES

The aroma alone of warming spices can lure you into a coffee shop for a gingerbread latte or a spiced hot chocolate. Now you can enjoy it at home! Just add a tablespoon to your mug before pouring over your hot drink of choice.

300g granulated sugar

1 tablespoon ground ginger

2 teaspoons ground cinnamon

1 teaspoon ground nutmeg

¼ teaspoon ground cloves

¼ teaspoon salt

½ teaspoon vanilla extract

1. Put 500ml water in a large, heavy-based saucepan with the sugar, spices and salt and bring to the boil. Watch carefully or the mixture may overflow.

2. Reduce to a rolling simmer and cook for 15–20 minutes uncovered, or until the consistency of maple syrup. Remove from the heat and stir through the vanilla. Leave to cool completely.

3. Transfer to a jar or bottle, seal with a lid and store in the fridge for up to 1 month. If your syrup crystallises over time re-liquify in a bain marie.

> **TIP** Add a dash to your latte, hot chocolate, pancakes, porridge or even cocktails!

TOWN HOUSE

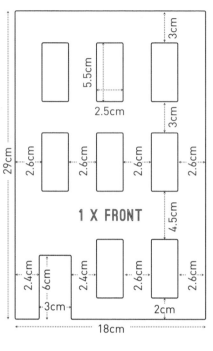

1 X FRONT

3cm

5.5cm

2.5cm

3cm

29cm

2.6cm · 2.6cm · 2.6cm · 2.6cm

4.5cm

2.4cm · 6cm · 2.4cm · 2.6cm · 2.6cm

3cm

2cm

18cm

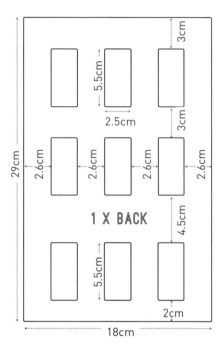

1 X BACK

3cm

5.5cm

2.5cm

3cm

29cm

2.6cm · 2.6cm · 2.6cm · 2.6cm

4.5cm

5.5cm

2cm

18cm

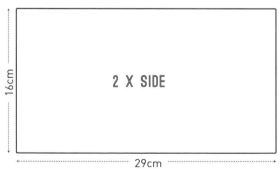

2 X SIDE

16cm

29cm

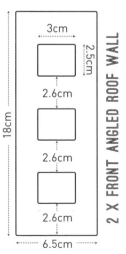

2 X FRONT ANGLED ROOF WALL

3cm

2.5cm

2.6cm

2.6cm

2.6cm

18cm

6.5cm

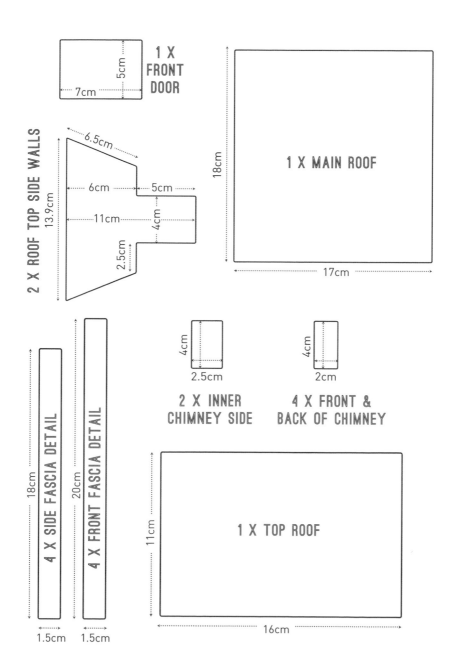

1 X FRONT DOOR

5cm
7cm

2 X ROOF TOP SIDE WALLS

6.5cm
6cm
5cm
11cm
4cm
2.5cm
13.9cm

1 X MAIN ROOF

18cm
17cm

4 X SIDE FASCIA DETAIL

18cm
1.5cm

4 X FRONT FASCIA DETAIL

20cm
1.5cm

2 X INNER CHIMNEY SIDE

4cm
2.5cm

4 X FRONT & BACK OF CHIMNEY

4cm
2cm

1 X TOP ROOF

11cm
16cm

HOLLY ROOF HOUSE

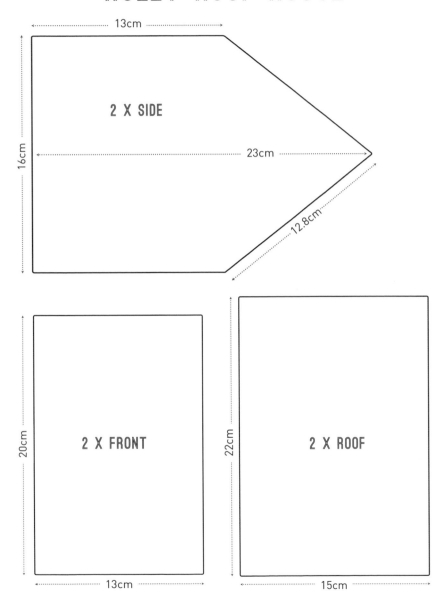

2 X SIDE
13cm
16cm
23cm
12.8cm

2 X FRONT
20cm
13cm

2 X ROOF
22cm
15cm

GINGER BREAD STREET 1

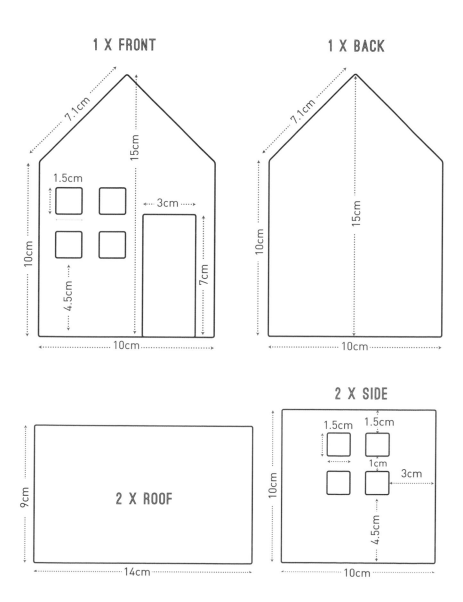

1 X FRONT

7.1cm

15cm

1.5cm

3cm

10cm

4.5cm

7cm

10cm

1 X BACK

7.1cm

15cm

10cm

10cm

2 X ROOF

9cm

14cm

2 X SIDE

1.5cm 1.5cm

1cm

3cm

10cm

4.5cm

10cm

GINGER BREAD STREET 2

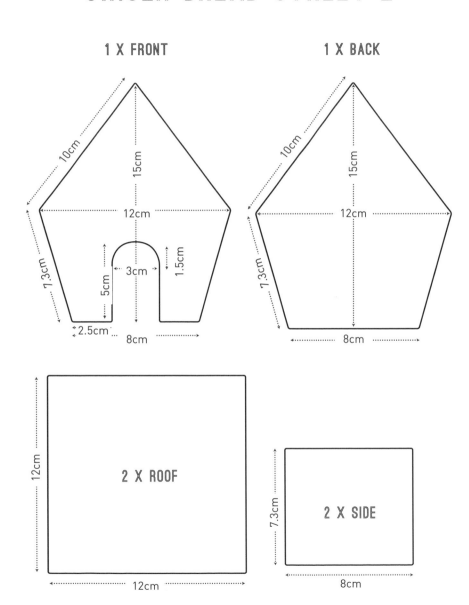

1 X FRONT

10cm

15cm

12cm

7.3cm

5cm

3cm

1.5cm

2.5cm

8cm

1 X BACK

10cm

15cm

12cm

7.3cm

8cm

2 X ROOF

12cm

12cm

2 X SIDE

7.3cm

8cm

GINGER BREAD STREET 3

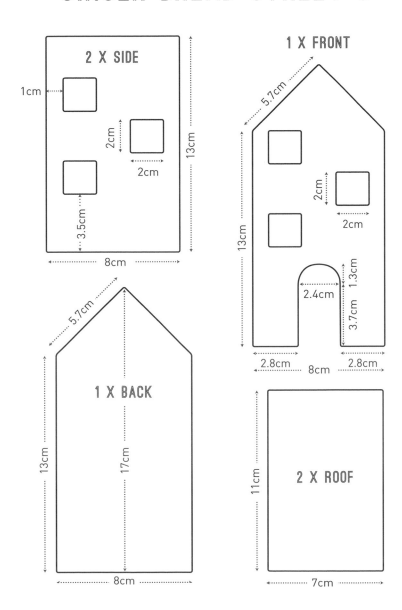

2 X SIDE

1cm

2cm

2cm

13cm

3.5cm

8cm

1 X FRONT

5.7cm

2cm

2cm

13cm

1.3cm

2.4cm

3.7cm

2.8cm   8cm   2.8cm

1 X BACK

5.7cm

13cm   17cm

8cm

2 X ROOF

11cm

7cm

HANSEL AND GRETEL HOUSE

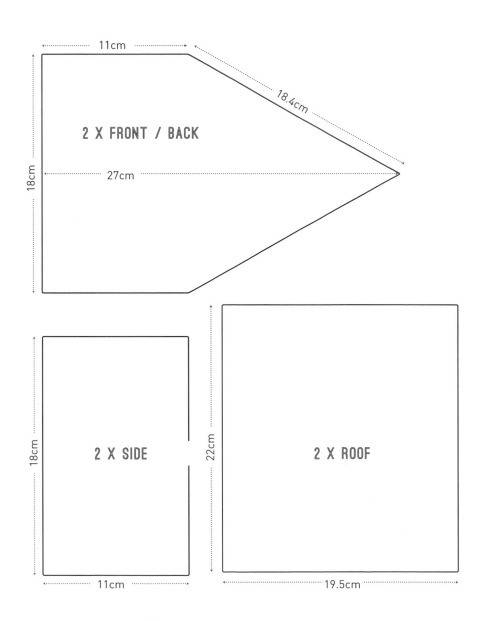

2 X FRONT / BACK

11cm

18.4cm

18cm

27cm

2 X SIDE

18cm

11cm

2 X ROOF

22cm

19.5cm

COUNTRY COTTAGE

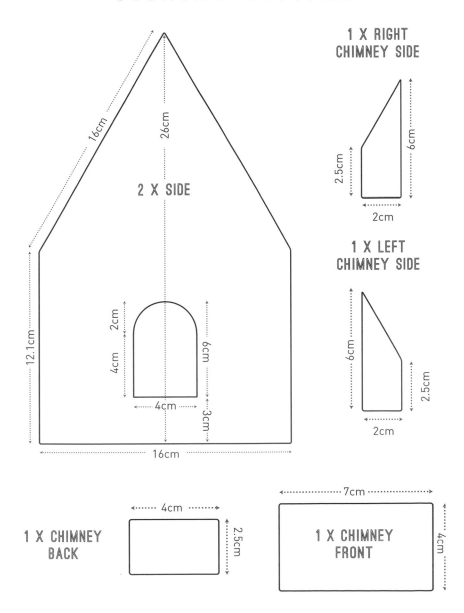

1 X RIGHT
CHIMNEY SIDE

2 X SIDE

16cm

26cm

2.5cm

6cm

2cm

1 X LEFT
CHIMNEY SIDE

12.1cm

2cm

4cm

6cm

6cm

2.5cm

4cm

3cm

2cm

16cm

1 X CHIMNEY
BACK

4cm

2.5cm

7cm

1 X CHIMNEY
FRONT

4cm

COUNTRY COTTAGE CONTINUED

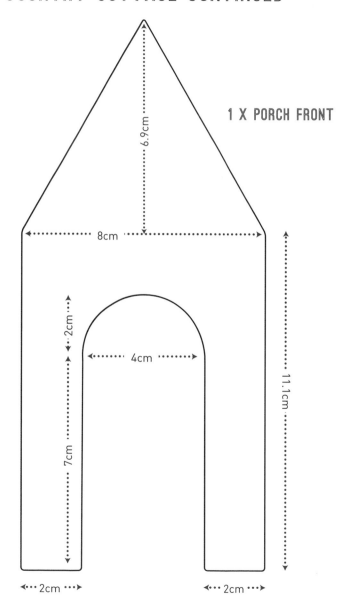

1 X PORCH FRONT

6.9cm

8cm

11.1cm

2cm

4cm

7cm

2cm

2cm

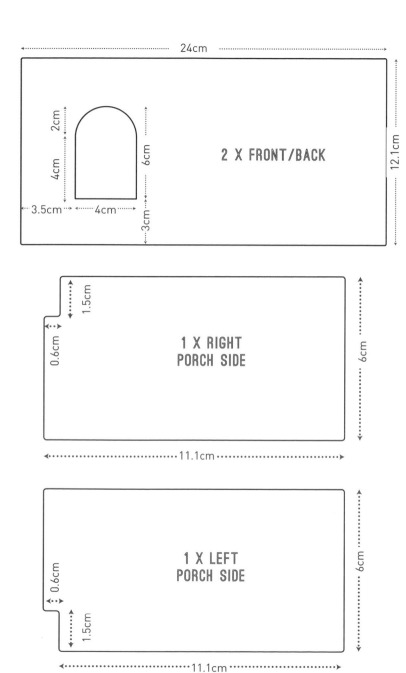

COUNTRY COTTAGE CONTINUED

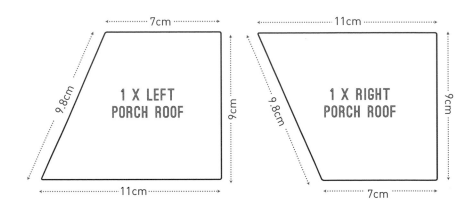

1 X LEFT
PORCH ROOF

7cm
9.8cm
9cm
11cm

1 X RIGHT
PORCH ROOF

11cm
9.8cm
9cm
7cm

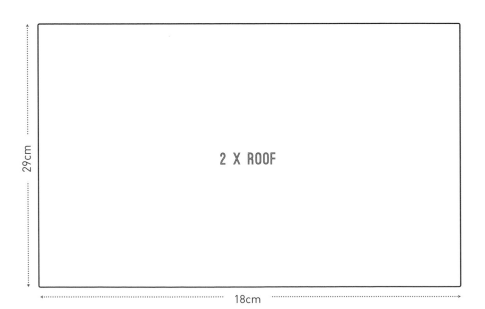

2 X ROOF

29cm
18cm

MINI MUG GINGERBREAD HOUSE

2 X ROOF

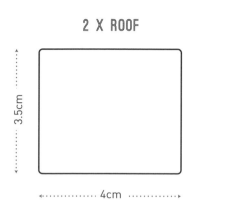

3.5cm

4cm

2 X SIDE

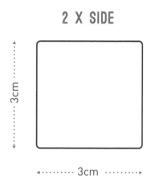

3cm

3cm

1 X CHIMNEY

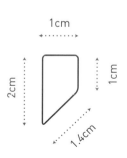

1cm

2cm

1cm

1.4cm

2 X FRONT & BACK

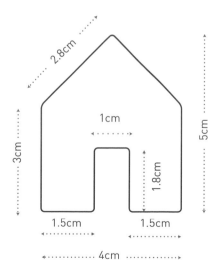

2.8cm

3cm

1cm

1.8cm

5cm

1.5cm

1.5cm

4cm

BIRD HOUSE

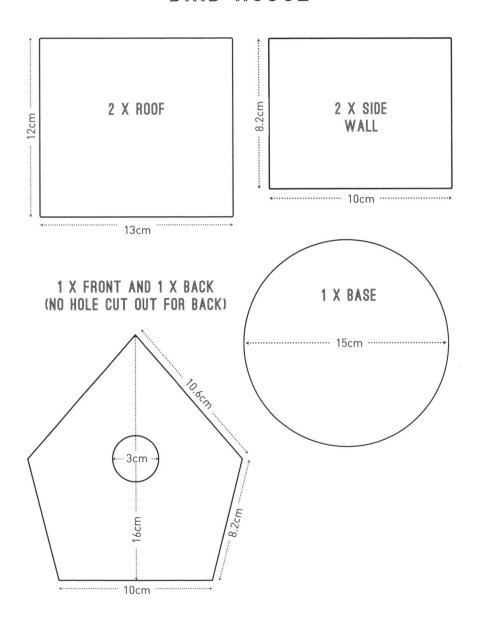

2 X ROOF

12cm

13cm

2 X SIDE WALL

8.2cm

10cm

1 X FRONT AND 1 X BACK
(NO HOLE CUT OUT FOR BACK)

10.6cm

3cm

16cm

8.2cm

10cm

1 X BASE

15cm

3D CHRISTMAS TREES

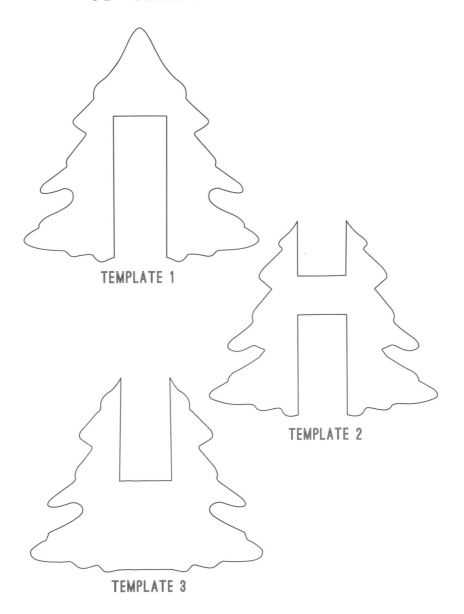

TEMPLATE 1

TEMPLATE 2

TEMPLATE 3

INDEX

THANK YOU

Many very talented people would give just about anything to have their own cookbook published so I feel overwhelmingly grateful to have been able to write my second book so soon after my first.

Some people gave their time, effort, advice and support, others just ate lots of gingerbread so I didn't have to look at the increasing piles any longer. Thank-you to everyone, however big or small you think your efforts were, they were huge to me.

To Kyle and Judith, thank-you for believing in me a second time. Your enthusiasm for new projects is infectious.

To Sophie, Judith and Hannah, thank you for your organisation – the work you juggle on a daily basis is really quite impressive. Your advice, support and flexibility have been invaluable to me, but it's your humour that is the key to keeping everything running smoothly!

To Tara, you effortlessly captured the magic that surrounds gingerbread. You produce the most beautiful images one after the other and I love each new photograph more than the last.

To Tabitha, you see the world in such a beautiful way and you have brought that beauty to life in the pages of this book.

To Anita, you have given this book the style I struggled to get into words when we started. I couldn't have imagined it better myself.

What a wonderful and inspiring group of ladies. Thank you for putting your hearts into it and for making the shoot days such a pleasure. Who said work wasn't fun?

And to Tom. For putting up with what felt like a whole street of gingerbread houses on the dining table and for laughing when I opened a draw to rest yet another tray of biscuits on when I found that every other surface in the flat was already taken. Your laughter and support is something I will always cherish.